Riding The
WIND
of The
HOLY GHOST

Riding The
WIND
of The
HOLY GHOST

BOBBI LYNN CAMPBELL

XULON PRESS

Xulon Press
2301 Lucien Way #415
Maitland, FL 32751
407.339.4217
www.xulonpress.com

Paperback ISBN-13: 978-1-66287-579-3
Ebook ISBN-13: 978-1-66287-580-9

Dedication

THIS BOOK IS dedicated to the Holy Trinity, the Heavenly Father, the Son Jesus Christ, and the Holy Spirit. If it were not for the operation of all three of Them in me and through me, this book would not exist.

A poem I wrote under the influence of the Holy Spirit concerning the start of my journey in the Lord of glory. It is called:

THE HOLY TRINITY

Who am I, that He could love me?
At the beginning of time, there was the Holy Trinity,
God the Father, Jesus the Son, Holy Spirit the Helper, all One,
Upon creating me, He sent me to earth and gave me a family,
A family through Blood and Spirit, bigger than the eye can see,
When he created me, He made my innermost being very carefully,
He called me by name, and said nothing would ever be the same,
Once I believed in His Only Begotten Son Jesus and what He did to save me,
This was the plan for me to be with Him for all Eternity,
I choose Him because He first chose me,
He drew me in by His Holy Spirit and now I am free,
Free from sin that once bound me,
He shows me every day how much He loves me,
He provides for me everything I need,
All is required from me is to seek Him and place my trust in Him faithfully,
He is showing me how to love and what it really means,
He is my Heavenly Father, my Lord and Savior, and my Counselor and Helper,
The Holy Trinity

All glory and honor go to the Trinity! "The grace of the Lord Jesus Christ, and the Love of God, and the communion of the Holy Spirit *be* with you all. Amen." (2 Cor. 13:14, NKJV)

Table of Contents

Introduction

Testimonies of the Father, through His Son Jesus, by His Holy Spirit.

THIS IS A record of the testimonies of His Holy Spirit living in the hearts of His born-again believer through Faith in His Son Jesus Christ and what He did on the Cross. The period of these testimonies is a time frame of twenty years. Throughout the years, many people whom I have shared these testimonies with have said, "A book should be made to bring hope to others and to show the working of the Holy Spirit in my life." That seed has remained in my heart, but I have not acted on it, until my brother who was just released from prison heard some of these testimonies and said a book needs to be created to bring hope to the incarcerated. When he said that, my heart jumped, and I knew that seed was about to bring forth fruit and it was time to create a book upon the Holy Spirit leading me. The Spirit bore witness with my Spirit that day to fulfill His Will regarding this. I pray this brings encouragement and freedom from bondage. I pray these testimonies of the Lord reach many all over the world to fulfill the purpose it was created. "For through Him, we both have access by one Spirit to the Father." (Eph. 2:18, KJV)

CHAPTER 1

Called into the Kingdom

HI, MY NAME is Bobbi Lynn Campbell; a born-again believer in Jesus Christ the only begotten Son of God, and the penalty He paid on the Cross for my sins. I am honored to share the beginning of my journey through Faith in the Lord. I want it to be known that all that is documented is regarding the Lord's good work, and not anything, I have done. He gets all the honor and glory! I want to give a little history of myself, so you can get an understanding of the walk of Faith, the Lord has had me on, and where it all began. I pray these testimonies of the Lord's goodness will bring great encouragement to you.

I am the youngest of four siblings, a sister, and two brothers. Our mother raised us, and our father became an alcoholic and lived in another state. I have a testimony that further explains in this book, about his state of living. I have never met him in person but have spoken to him on the phone a few times in thirty years. My siblings have met him throughout the years, but it was not a good experience for them. Our mom did what she could when she could. Some of our past is a product of not having grown up with a dad in the house to help her and for us to have structure.

We went through many hardships and loss in our years of growing up. My sister got pregnant at the age of sixteen years old and lost her baby at birth. My brothers have been in and out of prison over a thirty-year period. One of my brothers is battling drug addiction. It was poverty-stricken and life breaking and we never stayed in place more than three to four years at a time, pretty much life of a gypsy for many years.

I was out of the house at the age of sixteen years old, living a life of sin, drugs, alcohol, and jumping from relationship to relationship. I was married at the age of seventeen and had a son at the age of twenty years old. Over the years, I have been married and divorced four times. Not something I am proud of, but a product of not being born-again and living my life for Jesus according to His word.

After having my son, during his younger years, I made some bad decisions for my life and had my house shot up. I then lost custody of my son to his dad, and rightly so. I was encouraged to hand him over and felt that was the safest decision for him at that time in our lives. I was able to see my son during my weekend schedule, but I was still making very bad decisions for my life. One of those choices led me to date a very unhealthy man for a short time. He started to stalk me for about a year or so. He abducted me out of a public place, brought me back to his house, held a loaded gun to me, and put a knife to my chest. At this time in my life, I was not born-again in the Lord, and I did not realize at the time that in those moments that if he would have killed me, I would have gone to hell. Thank God, I was able to escape from that situation and move forward with my life.

At this point, I was only concerned about what I wanted and how I wanted to live. I did not think about how it affected my son or others that I encountered at all. I really lived as if I had no accountability to anyone but myself, a very selfish and self-centered way to live. "For the wages of sin *is* death: but the gift of God *is* eternal life in Christ Jesus our Lord." (Rom. 6:23, NKJV)

Years later in my thirties, I was visiting my friend's mom in the hospital, where I was employed for a time. My friend's sister was there with her husband visiting their mom as well. She asked if I would go to church where they attended that Sunday. I looked at my friend and said sure, if he goes with me. He said he would, and we made plans to go. She asked me a question that was odd to me at that time. She asked me if I cared that, it was a Pentecostal Church. I told her that I had no idea what that meant. She stood there and smiled and said see you there.

Of course, on my way to church I was running and breaking the law speeding to get there on time. I had my son for that weekend, and he was able to go with me. I slipped into the back of church and sat with my friend. I was not aware of what was about to take place in my heart and life. That preacher started to preach and every time he preached passionately; I became overwhelmed in what I call now Holy Ghost bumps. Yes, the Lord's presence was all over me. After he was done preaching the message God gave him, he opens the altar for people to come up and accept Jesus Christ as their Lord and Savior. I stood up at that moment and looked at my son and said I am getting on this train, and I am not getting off, are you coming with me? He was very nervous and said no, and then I looked at my friend and asked him to go and he said no. I could not get to that altar fast enough to make my commitment unto Lord. While up there, two women came to pray with me as I gave my heart and life to Jesus. I felt this load taken off from me. I have never experienced a peace as such before. The first Book of John says, "If we confess our sins, He is faithful and just to forgive us *our* sins and cleanse us from all unrighteousness." (1 Jn. 1:9, NKJV) The Book of Romans and Matthew go on to declare the following:

> "That if you shall confess with your mouth the Lord Jesus and believe in your heart that God has raised Him from the dead, you shall be saved. For with the heart, one believes unto righteousness; and with the mouth confession is made unto salvation. For "whosoever shall call upon the name of the Lord shall be saved.""

> Rom. 10:9-10, 13 NKJV

> "Come unto Me, all ye that labour and are heavy laden, and I will give you rest. Take My yoke upon you and learn of Me; for I am meek and lowly in heart: and ye shall find rest unto your souls. For my yoke is easy, and my burden is light."

3

Matt. 11:28-30, KJV

I was given a paperback Bible of the New Testament and started studying that from front to back, as many times as I could to get to know my Lord and Savior and how He expects me to live. I was still raw around the edges and did not know anything about sanctification. I was getting to know the Holy Spirit and how He operates in me. Many people did not take me seriously, but God never gave up on me. He continued to sanctify me and change my life from the inside out. As the inside of me started to change, there were changes that took place on the outside as well. I started to speak and dress differently. "Not by works of righteousness which we have done, but according to His mercy He saved us, through the washing of regeneration and renewing of the Holy Spirit." (Titus 3:5, NJKV)

One of the most important things I learned when reading the Word of God and during my growth in the Lord, is when we truly seek and read His Word, our minds are renewed. We start to live with a new mindset and the strongholds that once held us in bondage, are broken off from us. If you never read the Word of God, then you will operate in the old mindset, then that old sinful nature will dominate you and you will not grow in the Lord to maturity. When we are born-again, we get a new divine nature and it is important to yield completely to the Holy Spirit and renew our mind with the Word, so He has full control. The Book of Romans declares, "And do not be conformed to this world, but be transformed by the renewing of your mind, that you may prove what *is* that good and acceptable and perfect will of God." (Rom. 12:2, NKJV)

For the Holy Spirit to have full reign in your life, your Faith must be anchored to Jesus and to what He did on the Cross. Choosing to stay in communication with Him and studying in His Word so you can mature spiritually. A spiritual maturity needs to take place, so the Lord can use us and be effective witnesses for Him. When we are first born-again, we drink the milk of the Word of God, as we grow in Him the Holy Spirit will reveal to us the meat of the Word, as indicated in Hebrews below:

"For everyone who partakes *only* of milk is unskillful in the word of righteousness: for he is a babe. But solid food belongs to those who are of full age, *that is*, even those who by reason of use have their senses exercised to discern both good and evil."

Heb. 5:13-14, NKJV

CHAPTER 2

God Opens our Awareness of Him Speaking to Us

SHORTLY AFTER GIVING my life to Jesus and being born-again, Christmas Eve came around. I ended up celebrating Christmas with my momma a few days early. She blessed me with new blankets and bedding for Christmas. I stored the blankets I was using in a box in the garage of the place I was staying at that time of my life. Christmas Eve morning rolls around and as I was waking up, I was given a vision or a remembrance of a dream. At this time, I was not used to the Lord speaking to me and did not know what was happening to me. This was wintertime in Michigan and the winters there are cold and blustery.

Upon awakening, the Lord showed me a house that He wanted me to bring the blankets I had packed in a box to. I knew where this house was because I would drive past it every day on my way to work. I was not sure what I was hearing was from the Lord, so I reached out to a couple of mentors God gave me upon first coming into the kingdom. They came over and we prayed and a put a card together to give with the blankets inviting them to church. We also went over safety when working on similar things and remaining cautious. As the day went on, I felt a burden placed in my heart, which grew stronger and stronger.

I got into my car and started to drive there with blankets in hand, as I drew near to the house, my heart started pounding, and I was becoming nervous about stopping. I drove past the house and then said no, I will do this for the Lord and turned around and pulled into the driveway. I proceeded to get out of car and going over what I would say once, I got to the door. I went up and knocked on the door, a man answered. Before he could speak, I said, "This might sound crazy, but the Lord placed in my heart to come and bless you with these blankets." As I was finishing speaking, his wife was behind him enquiring of who was at the door. He turned back around and sincerely said, "No this isn't crazy at all." I handed him the blankets and the card, and as I was turning around to walk away, I saw the shock and amazement on their faces. God met a need and used me to fulfill it. As I walked to the car, the burden that the Lord placed in my heart lifted off me. That was the beginning of Him opening my awareness of Him speaking to me. I felt so honored that He chose to use me for this assignment. This strengthened my desire to communicate more with my Heavenly Father! I wanted to get to know Him, and I wanted Him to know me. I never had a dad in my life; this was my first connection to having one.

After this encounter with the Lord, I started having more dreams from Him. I always dreamt but the ones from Him were so different, they were in full color and detail. I started learning how to discern when He was speaking to me through a dream. I want to share a dream that He gave to me shortly after being a new Christian.

I started hanging around a friend that I used to party with before becoming born-again in the Lord. I was able to share with my friend my new walk in the Lord. She also informed me that she gave her life to Jesus as well. I was very excited and happy to be able to have her in my life in this new journey in Him. One visit we were having, she shared that she headed over a friend's house to have a couple of drinks and did not see a problem with it. In my spirit, I felt a warning going off. For nothing good ever came from me drinking ever. I left there and went home. That night God gave me a dream, a warning.

I want to share this dream and explain the interpretation that was given me. I woke up and knew right away that this dream was from the Lord, and was speaking to me through it. In this dream, I was with my friend, and we were at a skating rink. I knew that although this was a skating rink in my dream, it represented the bar we used to go to and drink. I felt very disturbed in my spirit during this dream about being there. I went to her and said we must get out of here; we are not supposed to be here. She had four children that were hers in my dream, one being a baby. She only has two living children in the natural realm, but in my dream, there were four children. She agreed and started to get the children ready to leave. I grabbed the baby and started to walk out of the building. What caught my attention in my dream was the baby was only wearing a diaper. It was dark and when I left the building to walk to the car. A car came out of knowhere and hit us. I was still holding the baby at this time, and I caught on fire and burned up to a charcoal, black color. My body in form but no details at this point because of being burnt so badly. The next thing I know is I am across the parking lot watching my body lying on the concrete in the dark. I was cut open from under my chin down to the end of my belly. There was someone standing over me holding something and I could not tell what it was. He leaned over my body and dropped what He was holding inside the opening of my chest. I went from watching across the parking lot, to sitting inside my body viewing everything being recreated. I could see new arteries and new tissues being created and the blood starting to flow through them. I woke up at that point and wrote it down. I brought this to the leadership of the church and asked if anyone could interpret this dream for me. They connected me to a mature Christian Pastor in the Lord, which was able to help me with that.

The interpretation this Pastor prayed into and gave me was this: "The skating rink represents the old way of living and the turmoil I was feeling was a warning of the drinking and going back to old ways with my friend. The burning of my body represented the old life passing away. The baby represented my new life in Christ, a new creature in Christ. The one standing over me was the Lord. He dropped that baby inside of me, which represented me, brand-new in Him. I was able to witness Him recreating me new from the inside."

The warning is this: I was warned being a new believer in Christ, not to compromise the new beginning He gave me with old ways of living. Going back into the past compromising my walk with those who are not walking that narrow path affected that. I decided to part ways with this friend; whom I love and pray for her walk in the Lord. I wanted to obey the Lord and not take any chances, compromising my walk with Him in His truth. My heart is fully committed to this relationship with the Lord and was not taking any chances on hurting that. I can only share the past with you all to give testimony, truth, and encouragement of what the Lord has done in me through His Son and the punishment of sin He took on the Cross for me. I can only account this by His precious Holy Spirit that lives inside of me and leads me into all truth.

We must always be growing in Him brothers and sisters. There will be growing pains, trials, testing and tribulations when maturing in the Lord. He also blesses us with love, encouragement, and blessings as well. The first chapter of James says the following, "My brethren, count it all joy when you fall into various trials, knowing that the testing of your faith produces patience, but let patience have its perfect work, that you may be perfect and complete, lacking nothing." (James 1:2-4, NKJV)

I had another growing experience in being aware of the Lord speaking to me. I was awakened at three in the morning, got up and grabbed my Bible and went to the table. I prayed, asked for understanding, and let it fall open. I read the chapter of the book it opened to and wrote it down in my journal. The next morning, He woke me up again and I proceeded to do the same thing, this happened for seven days. By the time the fifth day hit, I was dragging and not wanting to get up. I clearly heard in my spirit; "Don't be disobedient and get up" I got up and knew that was the Lord speaking to me and awakening me. That Sunday after seven days of this, I went to the church leadership and asked if they could shed some light on why God was getting me up every morning for seven days. All they said is, write it down and pray into it. All the messages that God revealed to me over that period had to do with the end times. Shortly after praying into it and waiting on the Lord to reveal why He had me do that, we had a guest speaker in the church that Sunday. He preached a message about one of the chapters I had read and documented. The next Sunday the pastor preached another message that I read and documented. This happened over a seven-week period with those messages being preached. God had my attention now.

The Leadership in my church at that time did not have much to say about it, so I went to a sister that was mature in the Lord and shared this whole experience with her. She said God was showing me that I was hearing Him and that He was the one getting me up and giving those messages to me. He was giving me confirmation when those messages were being preached, that I was hearing Him correctly. Our Heavenly Father loves to confirm His word in us and through us. Do not ever be afraid to ask for confirmation when seeking Him for something you are unsure of. Sometimes it is hard to wait, but He is faithful to show you. He wants to reveal Himself to us, which these are some ways He chose to communicate with me during these times. It is very important that we discipline ourselves to take time to listen to Him and ask Him to open our awareness of Him speaking to us. The Book of John says, "The sheep that are My own hear My voice *and* listen to Me; I know them, and they follow Me." (Jn. 10:27, AMP)

CHAPTER 3

Learning to Serve

I WANT TO make clear before sharing this part of the testimony, that the church is the training ground in preparation to evangelize and to labor in God's Field. The Ministry of Reconciliation is the ministry we are called into. I was so ready and excited to serve the Lord and get involved in the Church of God. "Now all things *are* of God, who has reconciled us to Himself through Jesus Christ, and has given us the ministry of reconciliation." (2 Cor. 5:18, NKJV) The Book of Psalms goes on to declare, "Serve the LORD with gladness: come before His presence with singing." (Ps. 100:2, NKJV)

I decided to start cleaning the church on a weekly basis, as I figured that was the best place to start. I did not pray, about where God wanted me to serve, I just jumped right in. Then my husband at that time heard that the church did not have bus drivers to pick up people every Sunday and then we decided to do that as well. Then we heard they needed teachers to teach one of the classes. I became my husband's assistant in that class. We decided to visit the Children's Church on Sunday to see if that was something maybe God was calling us into as well. Right away, we knew we were not called to run the children's church on Sunday morning, but we would remain teaching one class for a season. Through that connection with the Children's Church leaders, we were encouraged to go door to door with them to share the Gospel and invite people to our church. At that time, God was in the process of planting a big seed in my heart, giving me a burden for the lost and share the Gospel of Jesus Christ. "Then the master said to the servant, 'Go out into the highways and hedges, and compel *them* to come in, that my house may be filled." (Luke 14:23, NKJV)

Much growth came from this experience. I learned to seek God before jumping into any responsibility in the church or any ministry. He showed me the importance of waiting on the Him to speak, confirm, and open the correct doors. I ended up arriving to the place of not wanting to go to church, because I was overwhelmed and burnt out from all the activities, I put myself in. When we put ourselves into all these positions, we end up preventing those who are called to those positions from fulfilling them. Then we miss where we are supposed to be serving in peace from the Lord in being obedient. My heart was in the right place, but I stepped out of God's Will when I started choosing where I wanted to be. I ended up only having part of my heart in each task and not doing a very good job at any of the positions because I was wearing myself thin. If I would have only waited on the Lord to place me, then I would have been filled with peace and would have done a great job at the one position God has called and anointed me for.

God wants us to be trained to serve in Righteousness, and to have a willing heart to do it. Many people today just come to church but never mature in Him and seek the chance to fulfill God's Will for their lives. Every born-again believer has been created with a divine purpose to fulfill in the Lord's body with bearing fruit. "All Scripture is given by inspiration of God, and *is* profitable for doctrine, for reproof, for correction, for instruction in righteousness, that the man of God may be complete, thoroughly equipped for every good work." (2 Tim. 3:16-17, NKJV)

God had moved me to different church ministries to be trained in what He wanted me to operate in. Remember our foundation of being born-again is Faith in Jesus Christ and Him crucified. He builds upon that foundation and has you in training to prepare for the ministry He is calling you. Some spend years and years in one ministry, and some do not. It is all up to the Lord and His Will for your life. The Book of first Corinthians says, "Now you are the body of Christ, and members individually." (1 Cor. 12:27, NKJV)

Each one of us has a special purpose and function in the body. We have our own DNA in Jesus Christ, which no one else has. No one person can offer what God has anointed you to offer. Never compare yourself with others. You are uniquely made in the Lord, as stated in Psalms, "I will praise You, for I am fearfully *and* wonderfully made; Marvelous are Your works, And *that* my soul knows very well." (Ps. 139:14, NKJV)

CHAPTER 4

Baptism of the Holy Ghost

I ATTENDED A Church of God for around three months to start my training in the Lord. One service there were people at the altar receiving deliverance and healing from the Lord. I did not understand what was happening at first. Well, the mother of the son at the altar, the Pastor's wife took off running around the church speaking in tongues while tears rolled down her face, celebrating the touch that her son was receiving from the Lord. I was very uncomfortable at first, so much so that I decided to leave that church and attend another.

I started attending a Christian Reformed Church for a short time. I was water baptized there and was able to stand in front of that church and share my testimony before the baptism. I attended there for a few months. Something did not set right with me. I remember sitting in service wondering if there was more to church than this. I went to the Pastor of that church and asked him if he could explain to me speaking in tongues, so I could understand what was happening at that Church of God. He guided me to study the Book of Acts and to pray for understanding. He said it is biblical but he or the people in his church did not practice it. I decided to start studying the Book of Acts and praying to the Lord for understanding. God started speaking to me regarding where He wants me to be and confirming that I was not called to serve at that church.

I ran into the couple that initially invited me to that Church of God, and they asked if I would come back and give that church ministry another try. I accepted the invitation, and, in my spirit, I knew I was making the correct decision to go back. The Holy Ghost revealed to me, "This is the place I am calling you to serve for this time."

One Sunday a guest speaker came and preached a message in the church. He preached with such passion that ushered in the manifestation of the presence of the Lord. At this time, I was seeking the Lord to help me yield completely unto His Holy Spirit, so I could live and operate in the Baptism of the Holy Ghost. After he was done preaching, the altar was opened for those who wanted a touch from the Lord. I normally sat in the front of the church to get as close as possible to the anointing of the Lord as I could get and to be without distractions. When he opened the altar, I came as quickly as I could to get there, with both my arms held up in the air in complete surrender unto the Lord. Many came to the altar that afternoon. Two women came up behind me to pray for me. I was engulfed in the manifestation of the presence of the Lord at that moment. I was experiencing tingly lips and Holy Ghost bumps from head to toe. I declared from that moment; "I received my touch from the Lord."

At that time, the speaker heard what I was saying and said, "The Lord wants to baptize you with His Holy Ghost and asked me, do you want to receive it?" I said, "Yes, I do!" That was the yielding that the Lord was waiting on from me, so He could manifest His fullness in me. I wanted all that the Lord had for me with my whole heart! He proceeded to pray for me, and I went out in the Spirit on the floor for a while. I knew that a change took place and I was different from that point on. I had a boldness that I never had before. I started praying aloud after that and sharing more of the Lord with others. I was given a deeper understanding of Christ Jesus and the Cross. Growth in this new fullness of the Lord started happening. It is a different level of sanctification and closeness to the Lord. Even reading the Word of God was different; it is so alive to me, like I was there in person while all this happened. The Book of Acts declares the following, "But you shall receive power when the Holy Spirit has come upon you; and you shall be witnesses to Me in Jerusalem, and in all Judaea, and Samaria, and to the end of the Earth." (Acts 1:8, NKJV)

At the beginning of my walk in the Lord, I always prayed for the Faith of a child. After this transition happened, I believed with my whole heart, that I received it. I say this because most times, He had given me a vision and I was in it; I was only 5 years old. He revealed to me, it represents my faith in Him, the Faith of a child. I came unto the Lord fully yielded and willing to receive all that He has for me and welcomed the fullness of Him.

> "Then Jesus called a little child to Him, set him in the midst of them, and said, "Assuredly, I say to you, unless you are converted and become as little children, you will by no means enter the kingdom of heaven. Therefore, whoever humbles himself as this little child is the greatest in the kingdom of heaven."
>
> Matt. 18:2-4, NKJV

Years after attending the Church of God, it was time to move forward in the training of other areas that the Lord wanted me to grow and operate in. While I was in the new church during a worship service, I had a vision; My eyes were closed worshipping the Lord and Jesus walked up to me and stuck His hand in my chest, pulled out a swirling white ball, blew into it and placed it back into my chest. I was still in worship after He showed me this vision; I started to speak in tongues. God was giving me my heavenly language in the Holy Ghost. It started as stammering lips for me at first. I grew in that over the years and now I can speak many different languages in tongues in the Holy Spirit. "And they were all filled with the Holy Spirit, and began to speak with other tongues, as the Spirit gave them utterance." (Acts 2:4, NKJV)

This Baptism is for us today, as it was for them in that time. God wants us to live a life lead by His Holy Spirit in victory. I had someone come at me forcefully and did not believe in the Baptism of the Holy Spirit. I had lived in it for years and told her, it is unbelief that keeps her from walking in it and told her to "Step out and have the Faith to receive upon yielding unto the Holy Spirit." The first chapter of the Book of Acts says, "For John truly baptized with water; but you shall be baptized with the Holy Spirit not many days from now." (Acts 1:5, AAA)

The Lord revealed to me, that rest and refreshing come from speaking in tongues our heavenly language. Because it is the Holy Spirit inside of me praying to the Father things I cannot express. He takes the burden off from me and out of my heart and prays God's Will to be fulfilled. Rest, refreshing, peace and joy are the result of allowing the Holy Spirit to lead and intercede for me on my behalf. "For with stammering lips and another tongue He will speak to the people. To whom He said, "This *is* the rest *with which* You may cause the weary to rest," And, "This *is* the refreshing"; Yet they would not hear." (Isa. 28:11-12, NKJV)

I believe, at the same time Jesus was water baptized, the Holy Spirit came upon Him and baptized Him as well. He came up out of the water praying, the heavens were opened, and the Holy Spirit came down upon Him and the Heavenly Father spoke to them identifying that He is His Son. While Jesus was fully man; He was fully God and was our perfect example on how to walk as He walked and to have that personal relationship with the Father as He did. He was fully dependent on the Father and the leading of the Holy Spirit to fulfill the Will of the Father, with Him going to the Cross.

> "When all the people were baptized, it came to pass, that Jesus also was baptized; and while He prayed, the heaven was opened. And the Holy Spirit descended in a bodily form like a dove upon Him, and a voice came from heaven which said, "You are My beloved Son; in You I am well pleased."
>
> Lk. 3:21-22, NKJV

Just to share some understanding on some of these scriptures. I believe that we are called to go out unto all the world and share the Gospel. Additionally, when it talks about being baptized, there is the Baptism of Repentance into the Body of Christ; which is accepting Jesus as our Lord and Savior, repenting and asking for forgiveness of our sins. Water Baptism; which is an outward expression of an inward change and declares our commitment to follow Jesus, and the Baptism of the Holy Ghost; which gives us power to live a holy life of victory, to be a witness for Jesus, and to share His Gospel with others. This is our commission brothers and sisters. The Lord is still confirming His Word when it is truly being preached and shared.

> "And He said to them, "Go into all the world, and preach the gospel to every creature. He who believes and is baptized will be saved; but he who does not believe will be condemned. And these signs will follow those who believe: In My name they will cast out demons; they will speak with new tongues; they will take up serpents; and if they drink anything deadly, it will by no means hurt them; they will lay hands on the sick, and they will recover." So then, after the Lord had spoken to them, He was received up into heaven, and sat down at the right hand of God. And they went out and preached everywhere, the Lord working with *them* and confirming the word through the accompanying signs. Amen."

> Mark 16:15-20, NKJV

CHAPTER 5

God Provides Healing, Direction and Provision

ONE SUNDAY WHILE attending church service, my mouth was full of ulcers from having a low immune system, due to a virus in my blood. This was a new church God had moved me to for training in operating in the gifts of the Holy Ghost. In this Sunday service, I was in a lot of pain and was having issues focusing on anything. They had a communion table off to the side against the wall and had a few loaves of bread and a metal cup with grape juice in it. We could go and take communion of the Lord anytime during worship in that service. I had a prompting from the Lord to go up and partake of communion by myself during worship.

"The cup of blessing which we bless, is it not the communion of the blood of Christ? The bread which we break, is it not the communion of the body of Christ? For we, *though* many, are one bread *and* one body; for we all partake of that one bread." (1 Cor. 10:16-17, NKJV)

As I walked over to the table, others were worshipping, I had decided to partake and eat unto the new life God has given me through His Son Jesus and to drink unto healing in the new life Jesus shed His blood for. I pulled a piece of that bread, dipped it into the grape juice, prayed, and thanked God for this healing and new life that Jesus, His Son paid so dearly for me to have. As I walked back to my seat, I realized that all the painful ulcers in my mouth were gone, and my mouth was completely healed. It was such an intimate moment with the Lord. He showed me, He would be with me in all things in this new life He has given me. I just need to come to Him and rely on Him for all things. I have come to the place where I am completely dependent on Him for my every need and have complete faith that He will take care of me and lead me into all Truth.

He desires for us to come and commune with Him and cast all our cares on Him no matter how small or how big. He will be there to take care of it for us and walk us through it. We cannot do anything of ourselves to fix any situation. I have learned this the hard way. Now when praying, I bring the issue to Him and ask Him "what is He going to do about it?" Then I thank Him for taking care of it, even though I do not see the answer, I have faith, and believe it is taken care of. He is my Father, and I am His child. "Casting all your care upon Him, for He cares for you." (1 Pet. 5:7, NKJV)

We must have total faith and trust in Him in all things. Thanking Him for the solution before you see it, is Faith in action, believing He will move on your behalf. Remember, our lives are not our own anymore. We belong to Him, and He lives through us by His Son Jesus laying down His life on the Cross, which allowed the Holy Spirit to come and live inside of us after Faith is expressed and forgiveness of sins has been done. This is the most important decision anyone will ever make to secure their Eternity with the Father in Heaven, as indicated in the Book of John, "Jesus said unto him, I am the way, the truth, and the life. No one comes to the Father except through Me." (Jn. 14:6, NKJV)

The Book of Proverbs says the following, "Trust in the LORD with all your heart and lean not on your own understanding; In all your ways acknowledge Him, and He shall direct your paths." (Prov. 3:5-6, NKJV) He also gives us the answer to seeking direction in your life; this is the key to getting it. Are you acknowledging Him in all your ways? When our Faith is anchored in believing in Jesus the Son of God and the sinful punishment, He took on the Cross for us, then it gives the Holy Spirit latitude to work on our behalf. That is the only way we will get help from the Holy Spirit. Jesus must be the only Sacrifice, our Faith is in, that the Father will accept.

"But seek first the kingdom of God and His righteousness, and all these things shall be added to you." (Matt. 6:33, NKJV) This scripture guarantees provision from the Lord in all areas of your life. We must seek the Lord with our whole heart, He will then add to us not only what we need but also bless us abundantly spiritually as well as financially. Contentment in the Lord is necessary in all things.

> "And Jesus said to them, "I am the bread of life, He who comes to Me shall never hunger; and he who believes in Me shall never thirst. I am the living bread which came down from heaven. If anyone eats of this bread, he will live forever; and the bread that I shall give is My flesh, which I shall give for the life of the world."
>
> Jn. 6:35, 51 NKJV

CHAPTER 6

Mercy Given in Affliction

THIS TESTIMONY IS raw but still needs to be shared even though I am still enduring this affliction. This is a thorn in my side, so to speak. There are some things the Lord will allow into our lives to produce the fruit of patience and longsuffering. There is a purpose for it, and it may be different for each of us. Mine happens to be the Human Immunodeficiency Virus (HIV). Shortly after I was born-again in the Lord, I married someone from my past that also was born-again. I will add that the leadership of the church warned me not to rush into marriage but said to wait, pray, and seek the Lord regarding this union. I was told to date for eight months or so before making any decisions. We need to understand that the Lord chooses our mate that He has prepared for us, not us. It is important that we pray and get confirmation on whom, God is choosing for us, if that is even in His Will for our lives.

> "But the fruit of the Spirit is love, joy, peace, longsuffering, kindness, goodness, faithfulness, gentleness, self-control. Against such there is no law."
>
> Gal. 5:22-23, NKJV

Waiting was not something I wanted to do. We ended up rushing into this union and a few years into marriage, we both started getting sick were diagnosed with HIV. It was one of the hardest things to ever deal with and manage with a healthy mindset. It is truly no one's fault but sin and a product of sin from the past life we lived. There are things we will go through because, even though we are forgiven, the affects remained from those choices that needed to be dealt with. The Lord never promised this walk would be easy, but He said He would be with us to get through it. "The LORD *is* good to those who wait for Him, To the soul who seeks Him." (Lam. 3:25, NKJV) The Book of Deuteronomy goes on to say, "And the LORD, He *is* the One who goes before you. He will be with you, He will not leave you nor forsake you; do not fear nor be dismayed." (Deut. 31:8, NKJV)

This is the most important lesson I will learn from not being obedient unto the Lord and waiting for the person He had for me. Unfortunately, when I found out I was HIV positive, I was in denial for a few years and would tell people to get that shock factor to see how they would treat me. I was not treated very well in certain situations. Very unhealthy I know, but still it happened. Because I was in denial, that directly affected my health and my treatment. I would take medication to suppress the virus enough to bring my cell count to where I would not get sick, and then go off the medication so I could feel normal again. I knew the outcome of doing this but did it anyways.

The side effects were very hard to tolerate in my body. I have gone through many medications to treat HIV. At one point in my walk with the Lord, I decided to go off meds completely to claim my healing. I told the doctor, I did not want to hear what was on the report of my lab work, because it would affect my faith in believing for this healing. I let him know, I was not coming back ever again and did not need treatment any longer. After two years, my immune system was getting lower and lower, and I was battling many afflictions throughout that time. At that time, I was meeting every Tuesday for prayer at the church I was attending with other Intercessors. I would come in and explain what was happening to me and we would pray, and God would heal me of that affliction, and I would continue this Faith journey. In the Book of Hebrews, it states the following, "But without faith *it is* impossible to please *Him*, for he who comes to God must believe that He is, and *that* He is a rewarder of those who diligently seek Him." (Heb. 11:6, NKJV)

God has and is keeping me alive to fulfill His Will He has for me. He told me, "I will receive you home when you have fulfilled My Will for your life there." He said, "I have you there because you will share Me with others." There were times I was angry with the Lord for not manifesting this healing in me. I did not understand why I am going through this. I would pray for others and their healing would manifest but not mine. I finally came to the place that there is a divine time and a process for healing, and not to question the Lord in the work He is doing in my life, as stated in the Book of Proverbs, "Trust in the LORD with all your heart, And lean not on your own understanding." (Prov. 3:5, NKJV)

At the end of those two years, my sister called for an intervention concerning my health. My family members and I sat at a table and addressed how badly I looked and how my health was declining. Our momma was living with me at that time, and we needed to take measures for her care if I was going to continue this journey of Faith not taking my medications. Fear entered my heart and I decided to go back to the doctor and apologize for how I treated him and get back on medications again. It was not an easy thing to do. I had been fighting the good fight of Faith this whole time and was willing to ride it out until the end. I have others to think about and maybe I was going about it the wrong way. That is when I truly started to consider that God was bringing me through a healing process. I had such a peace wash over me and remain in me knowing He still has a plan for me.

> "For I know the thoughts that I think toward you, says the Lord, thoughts of peace and not of evil, to give you a future and a hope. Then you will call upon Me and go and pray to Me, and I will listen to you. And you will seek Me and find Me, when you search for Me with all your heart."
>
> Jer. 29:11-13, AAA

I went and tried to establish my care with that same doctor, He never treated me the same after that. My choices affected my relationship with him to be able to treat me effectively. I have been on a certain medication for some time now. Making those decisions, to come off meds and going back on, damaged my liver, and I now have an allergy to two set of medications. This limits the care I can receive, but all things are possible with God! I had to come off cholesterol meds because they were further damaging my liver. My cholesterol is at dangerous levels over 330. I have transferred my care to another doctor, due to being told my options are limited. I know God still has a plan, whether I am healed here or there. His Grace is sufficient for me. This is what He told Paul, when Paul asked the Lord to take away His affliction three times. This is my thorn to endure for the time being. I have a renewed hope putting my care in this new Doctor's hands. I believe this decision and direction is from the Lord. I am very excited to see the Lord work in my life and the testimony He is giving me through this. I believe there is a process for some and there are healings manifested for others. We must trust the Lord in the process of waiting for ours to manifest. It is producing fruit in our lives, and many will be touched by our testimony of it.

> "Concerning this thing I pleaded with the Lord three times that it might depart from me. And He said unto me, "My grace is sufficient for you, for My strength is made perfect in weakness." Therefore, most gladly I will rather boast in my infirmities, that the power of Christ may rest upon me."

> 2 Cor. 12:8-9, NKJV

Through having HIV, my compassion and empathy has deepened in my heart for those dealing with any affliction. My Father in Heaven is working all things out for my good through having this disease. My relationship and communication with the Lord are so much stronger and closer. I would not trade that for anything! I have endured so much rejection, reproach, and isolation in having this disease. I have had people that

I have been in a relationship with; want me to stay silent, because they were fearing what others may think of them having been in a relationship with me. I have had people stop me from coming over their house, because they were afraid of getting it. Many made a point to avoid or touch me out of fear of not having knowledge regarding this disease. I always keep in mind, not anything that I have endured will ever compare to what Jesus went through at the Cross for the sins of the world. What we endure here is only temporary and will end one day, when we get to our Eternal Home with the Lord. I will have a new body, completely healed and perfect! What a wonderful Hope to have! "And we know that all things work together for good to those who love God, to those who are the called according to *His* purpose." (Rom. 8:28, NKJV)

My biggest temptation having HIV was to come off all medications and go home unto the Lord. I fought that more than anything. I begged the Lord daily for a while there, to receive me home because I did not want to be here anymore. I am just being real and truthful. The Lord would tell me "I have you there because you are willing to share Me with others." That would be good for a while, then another hardship would hit me, and I would be back to begging him to come home. Finally, it hit me; I laid down my will for the Father's Will when I gave my heart and life to Him. If He wants me here, it is for a very important reason and when it is time and I fulfilled the Will that He has for me, then I will be with Him. I just got a Word from Him a little bit ago, "He is walking me up that mountain now." I will share bits and pieces in other chapters of different experiences I have had in the hardship of dealing with this disease. Please know that no matter what you are dealing with God will be there to walk you through it. He will never leave you, nor forsake you. He will work all things for the good of those who love and are called according to His purpose. He has truly done that in my life. I will be forever thankful for how close I am to the Lord.

"No temptation has overtaken you except such as is common to man; but God *is* faithful, who will not allow you to be tempted beyond what you are able, but with the temptation will also make the way of escape, that you may be able to bear *it.*"

1 Cor. 10:13, NKJV

The Book of Deuteronomy commands us to, "Be strong and of good courage, do not fear nor be afraid of them: for the Lord your God, He is the One who goes with you; He will not leave you, nor forsake you." (Deut. 31:6 NKJV)

CHAPTER 7

The Journey through Desperation

I WAS ATTENDING church service early to pray for the Pastors and leadership who would be preaching in service that Sunday. I was trained for Intercession in the Holy Ghost by other believers that were more mature than I in the same anointing, that God had given me to operate in. It was an honor to be under their care for that season. On this specific Sunday, my health was declining, and I was very emotional over it. I went to the back of the church in a corner that was more secluded, put my head down, and started to cry out to the Lord for comfort. I sat there, cried, and cried unto the Lord.

> "Blessed be the God and Father of our Lord Jesus Christ, the Father of Mercies and God of all comfort, Who comforts us in all our tribulation, that we may be able to comfort those who are in any trouble, with the comfort with which we ourselves are comforted by God."

> 2 Cor. 1:3-4, AAA

As I was watching my tears hit the floor, I had a vision of an impression of a big, golden bowl, which my tears were dropping into when they rolled from my eyes. I watched as a hand appeared and tipped this golden bowl over and poured my tears into this silver glasslike container. As I was still observing what the Lord was revealing to me, an older woman came over to me and started rubbing my back giving me comfort. She spoke to me and said the Lord sent her over there to comfort me. It was so comforting to have the Lord attend to me that way. He did not wait; He went into action and started to meet my need for that moment of despair that I found myself in. "You number my wanderings; Put my tears into your bottle; *Are they* not in your book?" (Ps. 56:8, NKJV)

I ended up getting a Word from the Lord through another believer. This Word spoken was, "For every tear that you have shed, it will be replaced with joy!" I was so encouraged with that Word, that I started to understand I was not alone in what was happening to me, I only needed to come to Him and trust Him to be there for me. I know He already knew what my need was, but He desires that personal, intimate relationship with us, and for us to have complete dependence on Him for all things.

> "You have turned for me my mourning into dancing; You
> have put off my sackcloth and clothed me with gladness,
> To the end that *my* glory may sing praise to You and not
> be silent. O Lord my God, I will give You thanks forever!"
>
> Ps. 30:11-12, NKJV

God uses His Word to speak to us, He also uses other believers to encourage us and meet our needs through His promptings. I have had the Lord speak to me through His Word, my thoughts, dreams, visions and through others that are His. It is important to fellowship with other sisters and brothers in the Lord to give encouragement and to get encouragement. Isolation is not good for any one of us. We need each other to function properly in Him.

> "For as we have many members in one body, but all members
> do not have the same function, so, we *being* many, are one
> body in Christ, and individually members of one another.
> *Be* kindly affectionate to one another with brotherly love;
> in honor giving preference to one another;"
>
> Rom. 12:4-5, 10 NKJV

This one Tuesday evening, I went to a prayer meeting very discouraged. I had written down many things in a journal that the Lord had given me in the beginning of my walk in Christ. It was a very trying time in my life where I was dealing with a lot of frustration. During that frustration, I ended up throwing that journal away. I felt conviction but was still learning in the Lord and did not heed that conviction. Over time I felt so sorrowful, asked for forgiveness from the Lord, and vowed that, I would not do that again. Although I knew I was forgiven, I still felt plagued with guilt and did not think God wanted to use me or communicate with me anymore after that. I went to a prayer meeting one night. I was sitting there in the corner on a stool, very quiet and somber. Some of the others that showed up at the prayer meeting enquired what was wrong, so I explained what I did and how I was feeling. They came over, surrounded me, and prayed for me. While they were praying for me, this sister in the Lord started singing a song to me that I have never heard before. She said she did not know the song, but the Lord wanted her to sing the lyrics He was putting into her spirit to me from Him. I was so very humbled by the move of the Lord, that I felt Him pick me up, dust me off, and restore me from those wounds that I allowed to separate me from Him. It is very important to hold on to what the Lord communicates to you! "The LORD your God in your midst, The Mighty One, will save; He will rejoice over you with gladness, He will quiet *you* with His Love, He will rejoice over you with singing." (Zep. 3:17, NKJV)

Some family members at that time and I decided to research the lyrics the Lord sang to me at that prayer meeting. We discovered the lyrics came from a song called *Come Away* from Jesus Culture. Even when I make mistakes, the Father is there to give me encouragement and set me back on the narrow path. The Father even takes time to sing to us when we need encouragement. I grew in these times and learned His love is an everlasting love. "The LORD appeared of old to me, *saying*: "Yes, I have loved you with an everlasting love; Therefore, with lovingkindness I have drawn you." (Jer. 31:3, NKJV)

The first Book of John says, "If we confess our sins, He is faithful and just to forgive us *our* sins and to cleanse us from all unrighteousness." (1 Jn. 1:9,

NKJV) Psalmist goes on to declare, "As far as the east is from the west, *So* far has He removed our transgressions from us. As a father pities *his* children, So the LORD pities those who fear Him" (Ps. 103:12-13, AAA)

CHAPTER 8

Coming Out of Your Comfort Zone

IN MY EXPERIENCE, the Lord will bring you out of your comfort zone, when He uses you. As you grow in Him, you will start to want and desire the things He wants and desires. The Word of God says we have the Mind of Christ. The closer I got to the Lord, the more desire I started having to go minister to the homeless, living on the streets. I will admit it, I was very uncomfortable doing it at first, but the love I had for the Lord overrode that feeling and I obeyed Him. "For "who has known the mind of the LORD that he may instruct Him?" But we have the Mind of Christ." (1 Cor. 2:16, NKJV)

A group of us believers got together and walked the inner-city streets of Grand Rapids, Michigan. We had wagons filled with bottled water, care packs, and backpacks filled with clothes and other necessities. We practiced praying for one another, with our eyes open and talked about how to deal with others who could be dangerous for safety precautions. We needed to take precautions in protecting ourselves as we are ministering to them. We wanted to prevent being robbed or hurt in any way. We needed always to be aware of our surroundings and have a prayer partner with us for accountability and protection when going on the streets to minister. "Commit your works to the LORD, And your thoughts will be established." (Prov. 16:3, NKJV)

We all went in different directions with our wagons filled, so we could reach more people to minister to. It was scary at first, until we continued to speak to people and share Jesus Christ with them. We just walked and when we stopped to talk with the person, the Holy Spirit would place on our hearts what He wanted us to pray. We came across this man lying beside a dumpster wrapped in blankets and had gotten sick by where he was laying. I bent down and prayed for him for deliverance and healing. My heart was so grieved seeing the condition he was in at that time.

We were able to pray for a homeless Veteran, that was just robbed minutes prior to us walking up to him, and had his glasses broken. The same men kept robbing him on a continual basis when he would go to the bank to get his money. They knew the times he would be paid, and they were waiting to get it from him. He said he was trapped there and could not leave, with no transportation and was homeless. We prayed for God to make a way for him to leave that area safely.

We prayed for a man that had his heart hardened from prior Christians that made promises to help him and did not come through with them. He said he did not want our prayers and he wanted nothing to do with us. His seventeen year daughter died two days prior on the streets. It was very cold on the streets of Michigan in the fall and wintertime. He was just wearing a t-shirt and it was cold and rainy that evening. We had been out for hours walking and we had one thick sweatshirt left in a backpack we were carrying. We offered it to him, and he could not believe we would give him one of our pieces of clothing. He accepted it and allowed us to pray for him from a distance. Once we met that need, he had, he seen we were not just any Christians, and that we truly wanted to help him and pray for him. "And the King will answer and say to them, 'Assuredly, I say to you, inasmuch as you did *it* to one of the least of these My brethren, you did *it* to Me.'" (Matt. 25:40, NKJV)

We came across a man that was in a wheelchair parked in a doorway of a store door, which was not being accessed. We stopped to talk to him, and he told us it was his birthday that day and that he was a believer in Christ Jesus. We started to sing happy birthday to him and pray for him. I bent down and saw the little worn, book that had half the pages missing and was dirty, torn, and stained. It was his Bible. He had the Word of God in his heart and was quoting Scripture the time we were there with him.

There were a group of gang members; we were able to pray for. We all formed a circle, held hands, and prayed for each one of them. There were discouraging moments, being yelled at from some who were intoxicated and aggressive. We did not let that hold us back, we just continued to move forward. We would still pray for them as we walked by.

We went out and walked the streets ministering to the least of these a few different times that year in the leading of the Lord. My sister, brother-in-law, momma got together with their Bible study crew and crocheted hats, scarves, mittens, and gathered donations for the care packs, and put them together, and sent to us to hand out on the inner city streets of Grand Rapids, Michigan. We also had family members here in Michigan that was sewing homemade cloth bags to hold their care packs in with other items they had to carry. We came across a group of homeless women to hand out those cloth bags to. As we were passing them out, a woman asked if we could get together, and have them pray for our children and us. We were shocked and humbly accepted the prayer. We met many believers that were homeless and needed much prayer.

We had an opportunity to share the leftovers of a meal that we prepared one evening. I decided to cook a big meatloaf dinner. I prepared enough for four people, but there were only two of us to eat it. We had enough food left for two people and then we were led by the Lord to pack it up and bless someone homeless with it. We gathered all the fixings and together with some plastic silverware, prayed for God to show us where to go and who to give it to. We started out our journey to the inner city of Grand Rapids, stopped, and asked many if they were hungry for some homemade cooked food to eat and they ended up turning us down. I could not understand why they were turning us down, but God revealed to us that some were scared that we could hurt them by putting something in the food and those were not the ones the food was supposed to go to. We could not find anyone to give it too, so we headed back and said we will look for someone on the way home.

A few miles in on our way home we drive through this under pass and seen a man sitting up under on one side. I said let us stop and see if he is hungry. Even though we had enough food for two, I was being drawn to this man sitting there by himself. We pulled over and started walking that way, and as we crossed the street, a man was on the sidewalk in front of us going in that direction as well. He stopped and walked up to man sitting down and sat beside him. I knew that moment these were the two men God wanted to feed with this meal.

We approached them and asked if they were hungry, and they answered fervently, "Yes!" We handed them the food and asked if we could pray for them. They accepted our offer and stood up to gather with us to hold hands to pray and bless the food that was given to them from the Lord. All four of us stood there holding hands in the under pass praying. It was so powerful! One of the men started to cry and that opened the door for us to share the Gospel of Jesus Christ with them.

We would stop and hand out Bibles for people who were walking, and riding bikes, to bless them with a small Bible, pray, and share Jesus with them. Even though we had a home church we were members of, we loved to go to church meetings all over the surrounding areas. We would attend morning and night services to be able to meet and fellowship with our brothers and sisters in the Lord and to get a touch from Him. It was so wonderful to have God pour out His Spirit upon us and bless us for seeking Him with our whole heart. There was a church we wanted to visit one evening and when we arrived there, the doors were locked. We pulled up and seen a man that walked there for service and was upset, standing at the door wanting to have church service. We told him we were on the search for another church to attend service that evening in that area, and he was welcome to join us, and we would bring him home afterwards. We did find a church to visit. God poured out His Spirit upon us and blessed us for bringing that man to church. These are just some of the moments God used us to minister to others in need, and through that, God ministered to us. Matthew says, "Ask, and it will be given to you; seek, and you will find; knock, and it will be opened to you. For everyone who asks receives, and he who seeks finds, and to him who knocks it will be opened." (Matt. 7:7-8, NKJV)

There is a purpose for your training and growth in the Lord. We are meant to go out to all the world and share the Lord and minister to them. I am so thankful God sent many in my path and still sends them to encourage, pray, minister to me, as He uses me to minister to them. We are in this walk together brothers and sisters in the Lord, as stated in Psalms, "Commit your way to the LORD; Trust also in Him; and He shall bring *it* to pass." (Ps. 37:5, NKJV)

I want to hear the Father tell me, "Welcome good and faithful servant, you may enter, here are your rewards and heavenly treasures for being obedient unto Me." We all have a circle of people that God puts in our path for us to reach, with our testimony of Salvation. We are all called into the Ministry of Reconciliation from the Lord as stated in the second Book of Corinthians, "Now all things *are* of God, who has reconciled us to Himself through Jesus Christ, and has given us the ministry of reconciliation." (2 Cor. 5:18, NKJV) Revelation goes on to say, "And they overcame him by the blood of the Lamb and by the word of their testimony, and they did not love their lives to the death." (Rev. 12:11, NKJV)

I believe the Lord places His desires in our hearts when we place our Faith in Him totally and yield our lives unto Him, He then establishes His Will in us. We will desire the same things He does. The Book of Psalms says, "Delight yourself also in the Lord: and He shall give you the desires of your heart." (Ps. 37:4, AAA)

Though He was a Son, yet He learned obedience by the things which He suffered. And having been perfected, He became the author of eternal salvation to all who obey Him. NKJV

CHAPTER 9

The Importance of Obedience

I WANT TO share a testimony regarding my earthly dad. I grew up without ever meeting or knowing him in person, though. I have spoken to him on the phone a few times while I was growing up. There was a lot of pain in my heart for not having him in my life; that needed to be addressed at some point in my walk with the Lord. God does not want pain and resentment to grow into a root of bitterness or rejection in my heart. When the time comes, the Lord will start to deal with us on the issues that have created strongholds in our lives, which stunt our growth in Him. "Looking carefully lest anyone fall short of the grace of God; lest any root of bitterness springing up cause trouble, and by this many become defiled;" (Heb. 12:15, NKJV)

I attended a healing gathering at a ministry one morning. Many were standing up and sharing what they needed healing for. Every time the speaker spoke, a motherly comfort would wash over me giving me such comfort and peace to my spirit. Before I knew it, the Lord brought me into a vision.

I was five years old (as I normally seem to be in visions God sends me) and was standing up and leaning against God with my right elbow on His leg. I remember looking over my right side and seeing Jesus sitting beside Him to the right. In my heart, I knew that I belonged to Them and was secure and loved. I looked down and felt sorrowful in my heart at how my earthly dad did not love me, nor was there for me. The Lord then spoke to me and said, "He didn't mean not to love you, the earth had perverted him." I felt sorry for him at that point and then was able to forgive him and start praying for his Salvation. "For if you forgive men their trespasses, your heavenly Father will also forgive you." (Matt. 6:14, NKJV)

When I came out of the vision, I did not know how long I was in it, but the woman speaker was still praying for those standing up seeking healing for certain issues. I knew I had received a major healing in my spirit, just sitting in my seat, from the Lord. At the end of the service, I approached the speaker and explained the vision and healing that took place during the service; how God used her speaking to give me peace and great comfort to bring me into this vision for the healing to take place. She was very encouraged and rejoiced with me regarding the work God just performed in my heart. "In this the love of God was manifested toward us, that God has sent His only begotten Son into the world, that we might live through Him." (1 Jn. 4:9, NKJV)

I was on a mission at that point to pray and intercede for the salvation of my dad so I could meet him some day in Heaven. This prayer lasted for about 2 years off and on when the Holy Spirit would bring him to my mind to pray and intercede. A few years went by, one of my brothers was out of prison at that time, and I went to pick him up and took him to church services with me. This one Sunday service, I asked him to stand in the gap for our dad to be saved and I would stand in the gap for our momma as well. I was not giving up on praying and believing God for their salvation and healing one way or another. "For God so loved the world that He gave His only begotten Son, that whoever believes in Him should not perish but have everlasting life." (Jn. 3:16, NKJV)

A couple of months went by, and I had trouble sleeping one night and around one in the morning, I had a strong burden to search my dad online to see if I could find him. Every few years that go by, I would do an internet search to try to find him, so I could reach out to him to connect. This night that I was burdened with searching for him was different from any other times. I put His name in to be searched and an obituary popped up with his name on it. The only reason I was sure it was him, was my grandparent's names were on the obituary and I was familiar with their names. I was so shocked and stunned that I went into grieving for days knowing now that I would never have the chance to meet him on this earth ever again. I was able to contact the place my dad passed away at and get information on him. The only thing they had left of him was his ID, so they sent it to me, to have something of him and see what he looked like. That is the only thing I had of him. They informed me that he was an alcoholic, which I was aware of from the information my momma would share with me regarding the past issues they dealt with. However, what I was not prepared for was the condition that rendered him in and how he was living for many years. They shared that he was homeless for 8 years living on the streets. God revealed that a year or so before he passed away, God sent someone from the House of Judah, a men's homeless shelter in St. Joseph, Missouri and picked him up. He eventually went into the nursing home part of that mission and passed away.

"The Lord *is* near to those who have a broken heart And saves such as have a contrite spirit." (Ps. 34:18, NKJV) My husband to whom I was married to at the time, did not know how to help me throughout the despair I was in, so he started to seek the Lord on my behalf and pray for me. The Lord gave Him a Word for me, and it was "Because of your obedience of going to the streets and minister to the homeless, I took your dad off the streets." I stopped grieving after this Word was given to me and was so very thankful. I believed God saved, healed, prepared him to be received home unto the Lord, and he is waiting in Heaven to meet me someday. I will be forever thankful that I did not let being uncomfortable stop me from obeying the Lord and ministering to the homeless on the streets. Now when I see someone homeless, I see my dad, my brother, or family member. I will do what I can to reach them upon the Lord leading me. Obedience is very important to the Lord! Now I fully understand why. "Blessed is everyone who fears the Lord, Who walks in His ways." (Ps. 128:1, NKJV)

Of four children, I was the one child that never met my earthly dad and was the one who discovered that he passed away. God had used me to deliver the news to my momma and my siblings. God gave me peace, healing, and strength in this whole situation and walked me through it. All things are possible when God is involved. When we pray for others, it does not matter the distance, for there is no distance in the Spirit. Stay encouraged and always forgives in all things, for the Father has forgiven us of our transgressions. "But Jesus looked at *them* and said to them, "With men this is impossible; but with God all things are possible." (Matt. 19:26, NKJV)

CHAPTER 10

Restoration and New Beginning

A DIVORCE HAPPENED after 8 years of being married to the man I chose for me, instead of waiting on the Lord. He had other plans for us in our lives. I do want to say that when we rush into marriage with the wrong one, we marry someone else's spouse that was prepared for them and not us. Then, we potentially block access to the one that was created and prepared for us. Plus we have entered an unhealthy situation being unevenly yoked for each other, and are in different places in our relationship with the Lord. In this situation, we ended up going our separate ways.

God gave me an opportunity through my sister and brother-in-law, to move to Tennessee for a fresh start. It was time to move forward and walk in the Will of my Father. When I arrived at Tennessee, my first concern was to find a church that I could grow and serve the Lord. I went to a few churches to visit but the Holy Spirit would speak to me one way or another to let me know which way to go. In fact, on one specific church visit the Holy Spirit showed me a vision of a water spicket dripping drops slowly. I knew that I needed to be somewhere where God's "Living water" flowed freely. "He who believes in Me, as the Scripture has said, out of his heart will flow rivers of living water." (Jn. 7:38, NKJV)

God led me to a Spirit filled church which allowed the Holy Spirit to move freely in the services. I felt I was home right away when I attended service. I woke up one morning and the Lord spoke to me as I was awakening and said, "I want you to pray for the Pastors and the ministry, this is an assignment." Throughout the years since being baptized in the Holy Ghost, the Lord has trained me to yield unto Him, so I could be used so, I could be used in Intercession for others and allowing Him to intercede on my behalf as well. "He who calls you *is* faithful, who also will do it." (1 Thess. 5:24, NKJV)

On that Sunday after my encounter with the Lord, I came to the Pastor of the church, introduced myself, and explained to him that the Lord has given me an assignment to come here and pray for him and the ministry. I asked if there were any other Intercessors that I could pray with and if it was ok to meet once a week to Intercede together. He introduced us and we set up a certain day of the week to gather in the evening for Intercession. We started to meet every Tuesday evening to pray. Intercession was very powerful and encouraging in the Lord. After our gathering, I would always leave refreshed and engulfed in peace. As I yielded unto the Holy Ghost for Him to Intercede through me, I would always receive a touch from Him as well. The Holy Spirit is so very precious to me! I do not ever want to take the gift of Truth for granted, and have been in constant communication with the Lord, since being born-again spiritually. The prayer never ends, commanded in the first Book of Thessalonians, "pray without ceasing," (1 Thess. 5:17, NKJV)

I want to recap a prior testimony; I finished the class I was trained in for Intercession. I was given a prayer shawl with the prayer of Jabez on it. It was the Lord informing me, "I have anointed and trained you in this and it is time to go to work." As a result, before I left Michigan, God had me give a person He had anointed and brought into Intercessory prayer, my prayer shawl. Now I really loved this shawl, I would wear it at times of Intercession in the Lord for the Pastors and the ministry. I was a little hesitant, but the Lord said He would replace it. I anointed her and gave her the prayer shawl in obedience and left. As I was driving down the road in Michigan just before leaving to move here, He gave me an open vision. It was of myself running on top of the treetops in long strides, as I stopped, I pulled up this big shofar and blew it. He then said, "This shofar would be used as a weapon of warfare." God also gave me a Word and said, "The most powerful weapon of warfare is Worship." I waited almost two years for my prayer shawl to be replaced by the Lord and for Him to give me my shofar. "For the weapons of our warfare *are* not carnal but mighty in God for pulling down strongholds." (2 Cor. 10:4, NKJV)

Now back to this ongoing prayer meeting with these other Intercessors. It was about two years into praying and the Lord said, "It is time to get your shofar." I was so excited but did not have a clue how this was to occur. I just happened to be going to Michigan for the week to visit family members. I was given a number to a man that gets shofars from Israel and sells them. I reached out to him, explained my vision and the way that shofar appeared in my vision, so he knew what I was looking for to buy. We set a time to meet on my way to Michigan. The shofar in the vision God gave me was a long, big shofar. I took precautions and let others know what I was doing and where I was going. My sister blessed me with some money for my trip, Which was three hundred dollars.

The shofar man sent me a picture of the shofar that he thought would fit the description of what I explained that I saw in the vision God gave to me. That is the one I chose to purchase. When I showed up, he explained that the Lord would train me in using it and give me discernment in the use of this gift. The cost of that shofar just happened to be the amount that my sister blessed me with. God had that planned out.

After he shared that with me, he handed me the shofar, anointed and prayed for me in this calling God gave me. As he was finishing praying for me, the Lord gave me a Word through Him; "I have prepared you for such a time as this." As we were wrapping things up the man asked me if I had a prayer shawl, I said, "No," he then threw a New Testament prayer shawl over to me. As I caught it, the Lord spoke to me and said, "I told you I would replace it." It was one of the most amazing moments I had experienced in the Lord! There is nothing more important than the relationship you have with the Lord, Nothing! The Lord always speaks to me and tells me: "Obedience brings great rewards." The Book of John says, "Jesus answered and said to him, "If anyone loves Me, he will keep My Word; and My Father will love him, and We will come to him and make Our home with him." (Jn. 14:23, NKJV)

I went to Lake Michigan beach and just stood out there blowing it and giving God praise, honor, and all the glory! I brought it back, took it to the Intercession meeting, and used it upon the Holy Ghost's leading. God trained me in all aspects of using the shofar and to use it only when led by by Him. It was used greatly in spiritual warfare and worshipping the Lord of Glory! As I matured in this anointing, God had me to anoint and pray for others to receive what He had prepared them for operating in Intercession. This prayer meeting started seven years ago and although I have moved on to another ministry, their Intercessors still meet weekly and pray.

> "Again, I say to you that if two of you agree on earth concerning anything that they ask, it will be done for them by My Father in heaven. For where two or three are gathered together in My name, I am there in the midst of them."
>
> Matt. 18:19-20, NKJV

CHAPTER 11

Sent Into the Ministry Field

WHEN YOU START maturing in the Lord, it comes time where God will send you in His field to be a laborer, sowing and watering seeds of Truth. God drew me to a business that Christians owned and ran. They allowed me to share the Gospel of Jesus Christ and pray for those coming into the business with needs.

I was walking into the ministry field and did not even realize it. I am going to share some details and testimonies of that work in this ministry field that the Lord placed me. One day at work a man walked in and God laid on my heart to pray for him. I went to the owner and shared with him that the Lord is drawing me to pray for this person and asked if it would be ok, He said "Yes," you can pray anytime, and gave me permission to share the Gospel of Jesus Christ as well.

God was about to start moving in this business and having free reign. He sent me there to be used by Him to touch others. I love God more than I care about what people think of me, so it was most important to me to be used by Him. I knew I had to be obedient to the Lord at all costs. I was created for Him and wanted to please God with all my heart.

The man God used to open this door.

I approached this man, very slowly and as I came up to him to ask if I could pray for him, he turned around and said, "I knew you were coming." I asked him if I could pray for him, he replied "Yes," I put my hand on his shoulder, asked God to touch him to take away his anger, and give him peace. I then went back to my work area to continue working. He came back up to me and said he felt so much better. This man eventually accepted Jesus in His heart started serving the Lord.

God is sending them in for prayer.

God started sending people in that business to be prayed for and to get encouragement. As I began walking in the anointing God gave me; I would give people encouragement, by telling them Jesus loves them, and to ask God to touch them. After some time of praying and growing, I learned to discern, what God wanted me to pray for in each situation and started operating in the keys of authority (loosing and binding.) After some time while maturing in my walk with the Lord, I started to bind up affliction and sickness away from people and loosing healing and peace as I was giving encouragement. God gave me understanding that the anointed prayer that I was growing in was strategic, and filled with power. The Book of Matthew states, "Assuredly, I say to you, whatever you bind on earth will be bound in heaven, and whatever you loose on earth will be loosed in heaven." (Matt. 18:18 NKJV)

Healing from nerve damage.

An individual came in with nerve damage in his back. I asked God to touch and heal the nerves in his spine, and the next thing I know he started to jump and down declaring, "I have been healed!" We were all rejoicing and thanking the Lord for this miraculous healing.

Healed from a migraine headache.

A woman walked in with a migraine headache and expressed that she was in much pain from it. I was drawn over to pray for her from the Holy Ghost. I asked if I could pray for a healing, and she accepted. She came back into the business a few hours later, and said by the time she hit the next store, her headache was gone, and she knew the Lord healed her.

God saved her fingers.

Another customer came in from having a lawn mower accident and expressed to me, they were looking at cutting two of her fingers off at different levels. I told her I would like to pray for healing not only to keep both fingers but also would be fully functioning. She came into agreement with me as I prayed to the Father with this request. We thanked Him for her healing, and she left. Sometime later, I was able to speak to her again, and she showed me that she was able to keep both fingers and was able to use them as well! I was so thankful she shared that with me. Not only does it build our Faith, but also it helps in stepping out and praying more when we are encouraged with the testimonies of God's goodness. Praise God, they looked a little rough, but fully functioning. I just pray, give it to God, and He does what He wants to do. I do not even have to see it; I just know He will do something.

Healed from infectious cat bite.

There was a customer that came in with a ball of infection on top of one of her hands. She explained what happened to her and that gave me an opportunity to ask her if I could pray for her. This infection she was battling was from a cat scratch. She allowed me to touch it and pray. I came against that infection, bound it, and commanded it to leave her in the Name of Jesus. That was on a Saturday, and she popped back in to see me on that Monday and said, the infection was gone, and that a complete healing took place. She and I both were thanking and rejoicing in the Lord.

Healed and delivered from Multiple Sclerosis (MS) symptoms and relationship restored with Jesus.

I encountered a customer bound in affliction from MS and could not stop her body from jumping and jerking. She was in complete agony, struggling to contain and to gain control of her movements. It was very clear she was suffering and needed deliverance right away. I kept observing her crying and I started ask God to help her, so I got up from where I was working and walked over to her as she was checking out and asked if I could pray for her. She allowed me too and after praying the first time, there was no difference. I was talking to the Lord and told Him, "Lord usually I don't need to see the work you do in others," but this time, she was still in agony, so I asked again if we could go out to the bench outside of the business and pray where we would have more privacy. She agreed and we walked out and sat on the bench. I asked her if she knew Jesus. She replied, "Yes" but there has been a lot of sin since the last time she served him faithfully. I encouraged her to repent, ask for forgiveness of her sins to be restored unto Him. She said she wanted that and proceeded to pray for forgiveness and healing. She also requested prayer for her whole family, so we lifted them up in prayer and asked God to touch them. After praying, we got up and walked back into the business. I did not notice it right away, but when she came back in and sat down to wait for her ride to show up, she was completely still! No jerking or jumping was taking place in her body. She was delivered when she repented and asked for forgiveness for her sins and was brought back into fellowship with the Holy Ghost!

Young man sent in for prayer by his mother.

There was a young man that was sent into the business by his mother for prayer. He approached the counter and asked for the woman that worked there who prayed. I said that would be me and walked over to him. I asked what his need was, and then we came together so I could pray for him. I was so amazed that God was just sending them in from off the streets to get prayer. God is so faithful to us, even when we are not faithful to Him.

Healed from kidneys stones and became a believer in Christ Jesus.

There was a man who came into the business that just left the hospital trying to pass kidney stones. At that time, I was over in another area working. He approached me and informed me of the issue he was having. He was in rough shape. The Holy Ghost prompted me to pray for him, but I resisted. I honestly do not know why I did not pray for that man. I felt the Holy Ghost grieve inside of me, because of my disobedience. I repented right away and asked for forgiveness and told the Lord, if he brought that man back in, I would not hesitate again, I would pray right away. That man ended up going back to the hospital that night.

He returned the next morning and said that he just left the hospital once again for the same issue. This time I looked at him and apologized for not praying for him the day before and that If I would have prayed for him then when the Lord prompted me to begin with, then he would not have had to go back to the hospital. I told him I was so thankful the Lord brought Him back in there, so I could have another chance to pray for him. I asked if I could pray for him right then and put my hands on the places where his kidneys are located, He said, "Yes." I went out, prayed in the Name of Jesus, and commanded the kidneys to line up with the Word of God and function the way they were created to function. After prayer, I went back to work, and he left.

He came in a few days later, and I barely recognized him, because he was not in his pajamas, and looked so healthy. He came over to me and thanked me for praying for him and said "After I was done praying a few days earlier, that when he went to leave, he started crying and by the time he got to the door, he knew he was completely healed and out of pain." He shared with me that he was not a believer until that healing came. That made him a believer in the Lord!

God pursuing a young woman battling drug addiction and asthma.

This encounter was with a young woman battling drug addiction. I would see her from time to time and try to give her encouragement and share the Lord with her. At that specific time, I had studied out of one specific Bible for over 10 years. That Study Bible was torn, taped, glued, read daily, and used greatly. The Lord spoke to me and said, "Give her your Bible." He prompted me to have her name put on the front of it under my name that was already engraved on it. I immediately went and had her name engraved under neath my name and cleaned the Bible up as best as I could for the shape it was in. When she came in, I approached her and said the Lord wanted her to have my Bible and that I had her name engraved just beneath mine. She started to cry, said that her mother is a Christian, and had been praying for her for many years. I was able to explain how to study that Bible and showed her where I marked the Scriptures about Salvation for her to read. She was informed that the only way to understand the Word of God is to be born-again spiritually, then the Holy Spirit would come to live inside of her revealing all Truth to her regarding Jesus and what He did on the Cross. I gave her the opportunity to accept Jesus Christ and get born-again, but she said at that time she was not ready to take that step. I knew in my spirit, that day was coming soon for her.

What the Holy Spirit reveals to us is based on where we are at in our relationship with the Lord. Some are babies in the Lord drinking the milk of the Word of God and some may be eating the meat of the Word of God. The goal is maturity in the Lord, operating in the fullness His Holy Spirit. There would be days that I would see her, and she would have her head hung and she would be covered in sores from smoking meth. I would always give her encouragement and prayers when this would happen and tell her to replace that bad decision with a good one. We lost touch for a few years, and she ended up passing away from an asthma attack. I looked up her Facebook profile to see if she ended up getting born-again and she spoke of Jesus many times in what she posted, which gave me a peace and a joy that I would get to see her again someday.

Salvation and sharing the word of God.

I had an encounter with a man that just had brain surgery, he was told, "There is no more we can do for you," and was given four weeks to live. I stopped what I was doing and said we need to talk. I asked him if he knew Who Jesus was, he replied, "That he knew of Jesus but didn't know Him personally." He allowed me to share in detail Who Jesus was and the sin penalty He took for our sins going to Cross.

When I was done explaining, I asked him if he understood what I said. He said, "I understand," so I gave him the opportunity to accept Jesus as his Lord and Savior, be born-again spiritually and live with the Father in Heaven for all Eternity when his time is finished here. I then shared the scripture:

> "That if you shall confess with your mouth the Lord Jesus
> and believe in your heart that God has raised Him from
> the dead, you shall be saved. For with the heart one believes
> unto righteousness, and with the mouth confession is made
> unto salvation. For "whosoever shall call upon the name of
> the LORD shall be saved."
>
> Rom. 10:9-10, 13, NKJV

After he accepted the Lord as His Savior and asked for forgiveness of sins, God spoke to me to give him my Study Bible that I bring to work every day. I was like but Lord that is my Bible. It was a new study Bible purchased after giving the one to that young girl. He spoke it a second time, I just sat there and the third time, He used my name and Said: "Give your Bible to him." I got up right away and was obedient, walked over to him and explained that Lord wanted him to have this to study God's Word and showed him how to study it.

Before I left work at the end of the day, a co-worker walked up to me and gave me a hundred-dollar check for another new Study Bible. I spent that amount on my Study Bibles. That customer ended up passing away two months later. I believe He is with our Heavenly Father now, praise God!

Prayer, Obedience, and Salvation.

We had a customer come into work a few times that I had connected with and inform me that her dad is in Critical Care Unit (CCU) about to die. She did not know if he was born-again spiritually and was very concerned about where he will spend all Eternity. She did not know how to share Jesus with him and that he was unconscious as well. I had attended our weekly prayer meeting that night but felt led to go to the hospital and pray for him. I went to the prayer meeting to prepare to go to hospital and intercede for this man's soul. There was an urgency in my spirit to get there so I left the prayer meeting early and headed up to the hospital with anointing oil to intercede on his behalf.

I knew someone in my past, who had leukemia, and didn't know the Lord. Therefore, she was not saved, and never attended a church. They had to induce her into coma for seven days to treat her. When she came out of the coma, she was quoting scripture and said a man came to her bedside every day and read her the Word of God. They told her, no one came in to see you and she said, "Oh yes, they did!" The Lord knew she was coming home and prepared her for that home-coming. She even gave them a name of the angel that God sent to her bedside every day to read the Word of God. She passed away a few months later. I wanted to share that testimony, so you know the mindset I had heading up to the hospital to minister to this unconscious man. I knew God could reach him spiritually and that He could hear me.

One of my concerns was, how I would be able to have access to the room, being I am not a family member. I just trusted the Lord to take care of that and knew if He sent me, He would make sure I was able to get in. As I approached the CCU, the door buzzed open, and someone walked out and then I walked right in. I found the room as a nurse was doing his vitals at the time. There were no family members visiting him. When the nurse was finished, she left, and around five family members walked in looking at me. None of them was the customer I had a connection with that knew me. They started to question me for the reason I was there and how I knew him. A man that was there was in opposition of my presence, but he did not say too much, I could just feel it in my spirit. I explained whom I was and how I knew their family member and asked if I could pray for him. They agreed that I could pray, and listened intently to what I was saying, a very intense moment to say the least.

I bent down and anointed him, laid my hand on his chest and started to intercede for him standing in the gap, asking the Lord to reach him and forgive him of the sins he has committed. Then I spoke to him directly and said please cry out to the Lord and confess your sins and ask for forgiveness and you will be with the Lord for all Eternity. I knew that he could hear me. I then asked the family if we could gather around him, hold hands, and pray for him, they agreed. They thanked and hugged me as I was leaving. The man that had an opposing spirit followed me out wanting to have a word with me. He was angry with the Lord for a personal issue and shared some of it with me. I was able to share a testimony of a healing, and he listened to me but did not reply. I knew at that moment a seed had been planted in his heart and would eventually be watered with God's Truth to bring forth fruit. He ended up leaving by the time I was at the elevator.

As I was waiting for the elevator, the customer I knew from coming into my work, opened the door to the stairs that were located near the elevator and walked out. I was so happy to see her and explain what had just transpired in that room with her dad and family members. I was prompted to encourage her to come back into fellowship with the Lord and renew her commitment to Him. She had explained that she was in a backslidden state and expressed that was her desire to be in right standing with the Lord and have that personal relationship with him. We held hands in the hospital hallway, and she repented and asked for forgiveness of her sins and was restored right there in the hallway of the hospital.

I went home; praising the Lord believing two more people that night came into the Kingdom of God! I was so thankful because as I was at the hospital ministering, the Intercessors at the prayer meeting were continuing to pray while I was there. God showed up! This is last part of that testimony. At the end of that week, my friend, and her twin brother decided to take their dad home, so he could be there with them when he passed. She shared with me that a few days after bringing him home, she felt a prompting from the Lord, to go in the other room to get her brother because she sensed time was drawing near. They came into room with their dad and started to pray for him. While in prayer she said, "A blanket of peace came down upon us as he was passing and, in that moment, that was my confirmation of where he went and also, I was able to feel the Lord's presence take him home." Hallelujah, Glory to God!

A few years later, that friend came down sick and passed away as well. I am so thankful she committed not only her heart but also her life unto the Lord that day in the hospital hallway. God is showing me the importance of being able to hear Him to walk in obedience living in this broken world.

Drawing her near and confirming her relationship with Him.

A sister in the Lord that would come into my workplace for some things she had to pick up. We would often talk about the Lord and pray for one another. She had some serious health issues that she was battling.

She popped into work on a Friday, and the Lord spoke to me and said, "Ask her where her relationship is with me?" I said, "But Lord she is always talking about you and praying." He said, "Ask her." I said, "Ok." then I told her the Lord wants me to ask her where her relationship is with Him, she declared loudly, that she loved Him and that He is her Lord and Savior!

That Sunday two days later, she, her husband, and children were at his father's funeral. They came home exhausted from dealing with that, and she told her husband that she needed to lay down for a few minutes. She went, laid down and about ten minutes later, her husband checked on her and found that she passed away. I did not understand why God wanted me to ask her that question but knew He had a divine reason for asking her that. I believe it had to do with preparing to receive her home unto

Him. God's ways are higher than our ways and His thoughts are higher than our thoughts.

Miracle healing, faith building, and more time given.

We had a brother in the Lord attending the Church that I am currently committed to, that is a truck driver and was not home very often. He made the effort to attend church service on Sundays when he was in town. His mom had serious health issues and battled diabetes. Upon coming home from working out on the road, he found his mom unresponsive on the floor in a diabetic coma. She was brought to the CCU in the city they live in. God gave me a burden on my heart during the week to go to hospital, anoint her with oil, and pray for her. I asked that brother in the Lord if it was ok to come up there and pray for her. He said yes please and that he might not be there because he needed to get something to eat. We were having church service that evening. I left work and stopped to get the anointing oil and asked for prayer that God's Will be done concerning her, and that I would have discernment in praying for her.

I grabbed anointing oil and headed to the hospital's CCU. Now, I am thinking it is starting to become a mission from the Lord to get to the CCU and pray for those who are on their death bed. I thanked the Lord for using me and allowing me access to these precious loved ones. As I approached the unit, I ended up pushing the intercom to let them know I was sent there to pray for that person. They buzzed the door open, let me in, and never asked me any questions. I was smiling at the Lord for His goodness. When I found the room and entered in, there were no family members in there at that time.

I approached her with anointing oil, laid my hand on her, and interceded for God to touch her, forgive her, and heal her. She was in an unconscious state, hooked to a machine that was keeping her alive, but I knew she could still hear me. I then spoke to her directly to cry out to Jesus, accept Him as her Lord and Savior, and ask for forgiveness of her sins. When I was finished praying, I thanked the Lord and left to go back to church service.

The next day the family was there, and they decided to take her off life support. When they unhooked her, she started to breath on her own and her heart grew stronger with every breath, Glory to God! They released her to the Rehabilitation Center two days later. She was given a chance to spend some time with her family and work on her relationship with the Lord. Months later, she ended up passing away. I am so thankful for that extra time she was given to get in right standing with Lord and spend time with her family before going home to Him.

Miracle healing regarding coming off life support.

Had another encounter with a young man that had a history of drug abuse but had given his heart and life to Jesus and was born-again spiritually. He was battling liver disease and damage from his past decisions taking drugs that hurt his liver. I would see him from time to time and pray and give him encouragement to keep moving forward in the Lord. Although he was saved, there were some issues that he would deal with and would be healed one way or another eventually. God had a reason for allowing him to endure these afflictions and it would work out for his good. He was in and out of the hospital many times fighting for his life. At one specific time, he ended up in the hospital on the CCU, hooked up to life support. He was on a waiting list for a liver transplant because his liver was failing.

Again, the Lord laid a burden on my heart to go to the CCU, anoint, and pray for him. I was talking to the Lord on the way there and said, "Lord they are going to start recognizing me in the CCU and ban me from coming." As I approached the unit, the door buzzed open, and some family members were going in and I took that opportunity to follow them through. The Lord continues to make a way, where there seems to be no way. I remember looking side to side and telling the Lord, "Let's get them all healed Lord and empty this unit." I found the room he was in and there was no one else in there, just him and I. He was hooked up to a life support machine and was unconscious. Earlier that day, they attempted to take him off life support and when they did, he started to decline and pass so they immediately put him back on it until the family members came in to say their goodbyes. I walked over to him anointed and prayed for God's Will to be done. I asked the Lord to give him comfort, peace and to touch the family members through this whole situation. After anointing and praying for him, I left and went home. The next day, they took him off life support and he started to breath on his own, so they discharged him home two days later. About a year later, he ended up passing away and went home to Jesus. I believe he fulfilled the Will of God had for him here, and when it was time, God received him home.

Prayer warrior and preparation for her homecoming with Jesus.

I met a precious little old woman that is a ninety-five-year-old prayer warrior in the Lord. She built a war room in her house that she wanted to have it blessed with anointing oil, prayer and the blowing of the shofar. She knew I had a shofar and had the anointing of the Lord to blow upon His leading. She asked me to come and be a part of that ceremony on a certain date, that I could be there and to bring my shofar. I agreed and was very excited to be a part of something so special. Another couple was able to attend to help bless her room and agree in prayer. She anointed the room with oil, we all came into agreement with her as she prayed, and I then I blew the shofar upon the Lord's leading. It was a powerful experience in the Lord with my sisters and brother in the Lord.

We connected a time or two after that until she came down sick and could not leave her house. Her health was starting to decline so, she reached out to me, and asked me to come anoint her, pray and blow the shofar. Before I went to her house, I sought the Lord on what to pray for her, how He wanted her to be anointed, and how many times to blow the shofar.

I set up a time, after the Lord gave me instructions on what He wanted done and how He wanted it done. I could not wait to get there to see her and bless her. Family members had to take care of her because she was so sick and could not get off the couch. She was however alert and conscious when I got there waiting on me. With the instructions from the Lord; I anointed her from head to toe, prayed for a peaceful transition and for His Will to be done, then blew my shofar twice over her, as I was prompted to do from the Lord. I fellowshipped with her for a while to give her encouragement, and then left to go home. She passed a week later. She was so precious and powerful in the Lord. I believe the Lord had me to go over there and prepare her for her home-coming unto Him. Everything the Lord calls you to do has a significant divine purpose.

Stage four cancer healing confirmation and an early home coming unto the Lord.

There was a very sweet lady that would connect with me from time to time at the place I worked that was battling stage four brain cancer. I wanted to make sure she was in right standing with the Lord and went out to the bench where she was and had a little talk about Jesus. I was able to ask her about her faith in the Lord, fellowshipped and prayed. She said she knew Jesus and had a personal relationship with Him. I was so very thankful to hear that and asked if could pray for her and come against that cancer. We prayed and, I bound that cancer up and commanded it to leave her in the Name of Jesus. We also prayed for comfort, peace, and encouragement for her while this healing takes place. She came to me about a month or so later and brought her phone in with her. She had a voice recording on it from the doctor, saying that he could not explain it, but her cancer was gone, and she was healed and in remission. She wanted to make sure she had proof of them saying that she was healed, and the cancer was gone.

The cancer was caused from smoking cigarettes. They told her that she needed to quit smoking, but she struggled greatly and continued to smoke anyways. This was a stronghold in her life that she was having trouble getting deliverance in. Smoking gave that cancer the authority it needed to come in and start afflicting her cells. She came back some time later and was very upset sharing, that the cancer had come back and was very aggressive.

The doctor told her the cancer was back and it was worse than before, and she did not understand why. I knew in my heart that I had to have a talk with her and asked her if she had stopped smoking like the doctor asked her to. She said, "I am still smoking."

I said the Lord can continue to heal you, but the problem is, you keep opening the door to the cancer. He wants you to be a good steward of that healing He had given you. We prayed for her to quit smoking and to be able to walk in that healing, but unfortunately, not long after that my dear friend and sister in the Lord went home early. I believe with my whole heart that anything the Lord blesses us with, whether spiritual or physical, we are to be good stewards with it. God had mercy and grace upon her, and she went home to be with Him. She was a precious sister in the Lord and a dear friend.

Miracle healing from infection in incision from having the appendix out.

A man that just had his appendix out, walked into my workplace, and complained he had an infection where they stapled him shut. I asked if I could lay my hand on the area where his affliction was and pray for him, he said, "Yes." I started to pray against that infection, bound it up in the Name of Jesus, and commanded it to leave this man. He thanked me for the prayer and left.

He came back a few months later and shared with those around him and with me, that after about ten minutes from that prayer, he pulled into his driveway, walked into his house and that infection spewed out from the staples that he had, and healing took place. He was testifying this in front of another person that he did not know.

That man had a ninety-five-year-old woman in the truck waiting for him, and after hearing that testimony, he requested prayer for her, and went out to the vehicle to bring her in. She had trouble getting around but approached me slowly for me to pray for her eyes. I said, "Most definitely!" I asked if I could touch her eyes while I was praying, and she said, "Yes." We prayed and they left shortly afterwards. I have yet to hear about that testimony. I just know God moved upon her and met her need. He is so faithful! She put her Faith in action coming into the building to receive prayer and healing.

Answered prayer in drug addiction.

A young girl walked up to me barely functioning, covered in meth sores. She looked so destitute and hopeless. I walked up to her and asked her if I could pray for her. She said, "Sure." When I went put my hand on her shoulder, she sunk into me and whispered in my ear that no one has ever cared enough to pray for her. I wrapped my arms around her and prayed for her. She left after that with tears rolling down her cheeks. She needed to experience the love of Jesus, comfort, and peace.

A couple of months later, her dad came into to talk to me and to thank me for praying for his daughter. He wanted to let me know that she was checked into a rehab center getting the help she needs, and that God was moving in her life now. I was so very thankful to hear that God moved on her situation and action was being taken.

Laborer in God's field.

Through this walk in the Lord, He revealed to me that wherever my feet are placed, that is where He wants me to minister. That is why it is so important to be led by the Holy Spirit and to act upon that leading and trust what He is doing. There comes a time, brothers and sisters, that after training and reaching maturity in the Lord, ministry begins. There are so any more testimonies that could be shared, but I only shared what the Lord had put on my heart to share with you. There will always be testimonies, when you have a personal relationship with the Lord and are being led by His Holy Spirit. Be ready and willing for the Lord to use you brothers and sisters, at any time and at any place He brings you too.

CHAPTER 12

Labor of Love

THIS TESTIMONY IS regarding my momma and the affliction of Alzheimer's disease that she dealt with in the last days of her life. The most encouraging thing I want to share is before this got bad for her; she had accepted Jesus into her heart and was born-again spiritually. I will be forever thankful that God drew her in and saved her. Her healing came when she went to Heaven to be with our Lord and Savior.

My momma was a meek, quiet, and sweet woman that knew how to love unconditionally. She had the gift of being a caretaker. God used her in caring for others, her kids, grandkids, her mother, and her friends when needed. We knew some things were not normal when dementia started to affect her memory and life. She battled severe depression as well, so when the disease of Alzheimer's started to progress, we could not tell that she was in advanced dementia until it was to the point of placing her in a nursing home for the care she needed. The severe depression masked a lot of the advanced dementia she was dealing with, so it made it a challenge of when to get her the help she needed and how to go about doing it. "She extends her hand to the poor, Yes, she reaches out her hands to the needy." (Prov. 31:20, NKJV) The Book of Acts goes on to say, "At Joppa there was a certain disciple named Tabitha, which is translated Dorcas. This woman was full of good works and charitable deeds which she did." (Acts 9:36, NKJV)

My sister, brother-in-law, and I were around her all the time, and made sure she was safe and had what she needed. However, we did not realize the condition she was in until she started to hallucinate and took off from her apartment walking down the road in complete confusion, without her walker, as her door was left wide open at five in the morning.

We knew we had to do something to help her, this was the moment of change that something now must be done for her to be safe. I called her doctor for some direction, and she encouraged us to bring her to hospital for an examination and place her in the Behavioral Health Care Unit for a ten-day evaluation. While she was there, they performed brain scans and showed us that her brain was shrinking, which caused the memory to disappear, and her health to decline. We knew this was happening but when you see it on paper, it made it terminal for us regarding the direction, she was going in.

We had to prepare and take steps that would get her the proper care she needed. We decided to try to place her in an assisted living home. That was fine for a few months, but then she decided she did not want to live there anymore and tried to escape to get to the highway. We attempted another assisted living home more secure but that only lasted a week and then she had to go back to the Behavioral Health Unit in the hospital, to see if we could sign her up for the correct insurance that would pay for her nursing home care.

God moved on her behalf and the insurance approved her nursing home care to be covered. She would be placed in a home that had a secure memory care, so she could be safe and could not leave. I made a promise to her when the dementia began, I would be with her until the very end and ensure she was taken care of. My sister, brother-in-law, and I all were there to the very end ensuring she was in good care. Of course, there were challenges, but God had a plan and took care of it as it came to us to deal with. She had moments she was aware of what was happening to her and was terrified. We said when we would visit her, we would make it as fun as we could, to help alleviate the fear and confusion she was dealing with. We knew God would go before us and take care take of her and us. "And the LORD, He *is* the One who goes before you. He will be with you; He will not leave you nor forsake you; do not fear nor be dismayed." (Deut.31:8, NKJV)

My sister and I would ride together to go visit her once a week and make sure things were going well. The supervisor is a Christian and did all she could to help us take the best care of our momma. The nursing home was offering to sign up for a class called, The Virtual Tour of The Brain. This was for family members to experience the limitations that our loved ones in that condition were going through. We decided to take part in this, so we could relate. A couple of our fingers were taped; we wore blurred glasses to show vision impairment and had tasks to complete. It was very overwhelming, and it caused us to feel much compassion and gave us understanding of what she was enduring. The wonderful woman that oversaw this class, sat down with us, and started asking questions about our momma's condition. By the time we left, God had her signed up for Hospice, which was the added care she needed for comfort.

She was on Hospice for a short time. They made sure she was comfortable and taken care of. I had been checking with the nurse every day on her condition and making sure she was comfortable, and at that time, they were closing the doors because of Covid-19. That following weekend came, and the Lord spoke to me on that Saturday, "I want you to fast and pray tomorrow for you momma." I said, "What am I fasting for Lord?" He said, "For her to loose her grip on this world, so I can receive her home." I said, "Yes Lord." Sunday morning, I started my fast for her to loose her grip on this world so God can take her home. I read scripture, declared the Word of God over her, and thanked the Lord for His mercy and grace. Around eight in the evening, I got a phone call letting me know she passed away. I shared with the nurse that the Lord had called me to a fast for her, so He could receive her home. The nurse told me she passed peacefully. While that nurse was tending to my momma, there was another person that passed away as well. Jesus was receiving His children at home.

I wanted to share this testimony, so you can see the care that the Lord took concerning my momma and her affliction. He not only took such loving care of her, but He made the decisions that needed to be made for end-of-life care and then when the time came, He called me to pray for her so she could go home unto Him. I did not share all the details throughout the journey, but I wanted to give the ones encouragement that are on that same journey with their loved ones. Please know that when you surrender all unto the Lord, He will not only care for your loved ones but also ensure the decisions made for them are taken care of to give you peace and comfort during it. Trust the Lord in this He will not fail you. "Fear not, for I *am* with you; Be not dismayed, for I *am* your God. I will strengthen you, Yes, I will help you, I will uphold you with My righteous right hand.'" (Isa. 41:10, NKJV) The Book of Philippians moves forward to say, "And my God shall supply all your need according to His riches in glory by Christ Jesus." (Phil. 4:19, NKJV)

CHAPTER 13

The Ministry God Called Me to Serve In

HARDCORE DISCIPLES OF Jesus Christ Biker Church is the ministry God called me to serve during this season of my walk in Him. The Pastor's name is Preacher Ray Slater. God uses this ministry in preaching the Gospel of Jesus Christ and reaching the least of these. Most of the members are former substance abusers, bikers, and have been in prisons or jails in their past lives that are born-again believers now. Several hard-core individuals are involved in this ministry that love the Lord with all their hearts. This ministry also has social media classes that deal with addiction recovery. This ministry has blessed me in serving and I have grown a lot from being a part of it. I am the Intercessor, Pastor of Prayer, and Teacher for the Children's Church. "And He Himself gave some *to be* apostles, some prophets, some evangelists, and some pastors and teachers, for the equipping of the saints for the work of ministry, for the edifying of the body of Christ." (Eph. 4:11-12, NKJV)

My boss came to me during 2018 and said he wanted me to meet Preacher Ray Slater and work with him to help people that were battling drug addiction. I had an opportunity to connect people to Preacher Ray, that were battling addiction that I was aware of, to send them to rehab centers all around the United States. I only connected those with him that truly wanted to be delivered and stay clean. This ministry and the believers in this ministry believe the only way to receive deliverance and stay clean is being born-again spiritually with our Faith anchored in Jesus Christ and what He did at the Cross. There were some successes and some that did not believe or want to stay clean. God has brought this ministry in a direction that does not place people into rehab centers anymore, but we will still put people in the right direction for a Faith based Rehabilitation Center and who to contact. I am very grateful for the connection the Lord established with Preacher Ray and I through Him to serve in the same ministry for such a time as this.

> "Let us hold fast the confession of *our* hope without wavering, for He who promised *is* faithful. And let us consider one another in order to stir up love and good works, not forsaking the assembling of ourselves together, as *is* the manner of some, but exhorting *one another*, and so much the more as you see the Day approaching."

Heb. 10:23-25, NJKV

Preacher Ray and Associate Pastor Joshua would go out different days of the week, preach the Word of God at the community kitchen for the homeless, and walk the streets in town sharing the Gospel of Jesus Christ praying for them. A large social media platform follows this ministry throughout the United States and many other Countries. "Preach the Word! Be ready in season *and* out of season. Convince, rebuke, exhort, with all longsuffering and teaching." (2 Tim. 4:2, NKJV)

As the years pass by and times are changing living during the end times, God is starting to move this ministry into being a fulltime online church media and many people are being reached. He has a remnant of disciples in leadership in the ministry that help him. We are a close family knitted in love that serve together to give God Glory in all we do. I will serve here until the Lord directs me otherwise. I encourage you to pray and allow God to lead you to get involved into a ministry where you can become one with that part of the body to serve Him in love.

"And you shall love the LORD your God with all your heart, and with all your soul, and with all your mind, and with all your strength.' This *is* the first commandment. And the second, like *it, is* this: 'You shall love your neighbor as yourself.' There is no other commandment greater than these."

Mark 12:30-31, NKJV

CHAPTER 14

The Testimony of Preacher Ray Slater and The Hardcore Disciples of Jesus Christ Biker Church

I AM HONORED to be able to share some of Preacher Ray's testimony with you to understand the type of anointing God has upon his life. He endured much abuse as a child and upon growing up came into the biker lifestyle for most of his life. Years ago, before being born-again spiritually, he tried to live a peaceful life of doing the right thing and take care of his family. He had his own construction business for many years; however, things were just not working out for him.

He eventually made the decision to start a new life under another alias, "Sonny." He moved his family out of the house and moved to another state, opened, and ran a few tattoo businesses and became a cocaine dealer. He was caught up in running bars and living in lust with many women. That lifestyle lasted for many years until the law caught up to him. He was busted and incarcerated in the federal prison system for 5 years of his life. He did get promptings from the Lord, that he should not being living this way, but ignored them. The Holy Spirit was trying to draw him in many times throughout living his sinful lifestyle. "For the wages of sin *is* death, but the gift of God is eternal life in Christ Jesus our Lord." (Rom. 6:23, NKJV)

Coming out of prison, he was able to go back into the tattoo business for a living. The people he had employed kept things running for him when he was in prison. The business was not what it was when he first went into prison. God started to speak to his spirit and prompting him to find a church. He decided it was time to find a church to attend, so he opened the phone book, searched for a church to attend, called and spoke to the Pastor. The Pastor wanted to know about him and his past. He shared it all with this Pastor, ALL of it. After that conversation was done, the Pastor said to him, that they had nothing for him there at his church. He could refer him to a church for people like him. Yes, this Pastor rejected him from coming to his church. Preacher Ray had not even given his life to Christ just yet but felt led to find a church to attend. "For we do not wrestle against flesh and blood, but against principalities, against powers, against the rulers of the darkness of this age, against spiritual *hosts* of wickedness in the heavenly *places*." (Eph. 6:12, NKJV)

He decided to go to the church that he was referred to for people like him. Thank God, they had a Pastor there that embraced him and took him in. One service the Holy Spirit worked on his heart and drew him to the altar in 2001 to surrender his life to the Lord. He slowly made his way down that isle to the altar, throwing off his cap, coat, vest, and dropped to his knees at the steps, fell out in the Spirit, and laid there for hours. He woke up hours later and no one was left in the church. He knew that he knew with all that was in his being that God saved him and redeemed him from his sin.

He continued to work as a tattoo artist for some time after being born-again spiritually. He got involved in the men's ministry at that church he was attending. He was being trained for ministry for five years under his Pastor's care. When the time came for him to leave this ministry and start one that God had for him, God closed that door and opened a new one. He also at that time told him, it was time for him to stop doing tattoos, because God saved him for more than that. At that time, a seed was planted in Preacher Ray's heart to go fulltime in the ministry of Hardcore Disciples of Jesus Christ Biker Church. He has endured much persecution over the years in this ministry. "You therefore must endure hardship as a good soldier of Jesus Christ. No one engaged in warfare entangles himself with the affairs of *this* life, that he may please him who enlisted him as a soldier." (2 Tim. 2:3-4, NKJV)

God started pouring the details for ministry and how it should be managed. Preacher Ray has put in much prayer, years of growth, and pruning in this ministry. It has been 23 years since this ministry was birthed through him by the Holy Spirit and is still in operation and going strong. This ministry is for people with backgrounds and pasts that would not be accepted by most churches today. It is for the least of these, like me. We have many members that find refuge, peace, and healing in this part of the Body of Christ. I will be forever thankful, for God calling this man into a ministry for people like us. This ministry is growing on social media all over the United States and in many other countries. If you have an opportunity to be a part of it, you can watch it online and get the preaching of the Word of God, encouragement, prayer and connection to other brothers and sisters all over the world. You will be welcomed! You can access us on the Hardcore Disciples of Jesus Christ media page on Facebook or his personal Ray Slater page on Facebook. "Obey those who rule over you, and be submissive, for they watch out for your souls, as those who must give an account. Let them do so with joy and not with grief, for that would be unprofitable for you." (Heb. 13:17, NKJV)

There was so much more to his testimony that I could not share but was thankful to hear what God has done in this man's life and that I was able to share it with you. I believe God has given Preacher Ray an Evangelist and Watchman calling upon his life. He sounds the alarm day and night preaching the Word of God trying to reach the many. He can always be contacted on Facebook Messenger. He does a pod cast at 5:00am every morning, online devotion mornings at 7:00am, evening online classes at 7:00pm Monday through Friday, and Sunday online church service can be viewed at 11: 45am. Take care and God bless each of you. "But you be watchful in all things, endure afflictions, do the work of an evangelist, fulfill your ministry." (2 Tim. 4:5, NKJV)

Holy Testimony

Holy, Jesus You are Holy, Holy, You are my Majesty,
The perfect Sacrifice, willing to lay down His life, for all of humanity,
Taking back the keys, of our God given authority,
Rising from the dead, just like God said,
So we could be with Him for all eternity,
Surrender your hearts, and believe, in His Holy Testimony, and be free,
Holy, Jesus You are Holy, Holy, You are my King of Kings,
Perfect Lamb of God, says He loves me, He laid down His life,
for me and my family,
He cleansed my heart, and purified me,
His precious Holy Spirit, then came inside me,
Faith is the key, in believing, in His Holy Testimony, and being free,
So do not turn away, your heart from Him, He is the light in this world
that will never grow dim,
Ancient of Days, The Great I AM, Jehovah Jireh,
The Beginning and The End,
Body, soul, and spirit, all cry to Him, waiting for the time,
of the world to end,
So do not waste any time, just believe in His Holy Testimony and be free,
Holy, Jesus You are Holy, Holy, You are my King of Kings

Eternity

I WAS PUTTING my grandson to bed one evening, and we would always praise the Lord, thank Him, and then pray every night before tucking him into his covers to go to sleep. On this evening, shortly after praising the Lord, a message started coming forth from Him. It is called:

Eternity

I lift up my voice to praise You.
You are the only One who knows me.
I will love You for all Eternity.
You are the Alpha and Omega, my High Tower that can calm a raging sea.

"Look to me forever, I have a place for you for all Eternity,
You are My creation and My beloved, whom My Son had to pay a
great fee,
Do not turn away from Him or you will live in misery for all Eternity,
My Love is real and all you need is the Faith of a mustard seed,
I am All-Powerful and nothing is lacking,
My Heart breaks for my people, because they have blinders on their eyes
that they choose not to see,
Humble yourself before Me and I will lift you up for all Eternity,
Eternity is forever, so choose wisely and give your heart to Me!"

ACKNOWLEDGEMENTS

I GIVE ALL the Glory to God the Father, Jesus the Son, and the Holy Spirit the Helper! Without Them, this book would not even exist. I want to thank my brother-in-law for allowing me to help create the book cover, my sister Susan for loving and encouraging me to continue in this life, my brother George for encouraging me to write this book, to my son Nikolaus for always being there, praying for me and encouraging me to move forward in this journey, to Preacher Ray for your testimony, friendship, and prayers, to my brother in the Lord, David for drawing three of the pictures for this book, for your friendship and prayers. I also want to thank Xulon Publishing for taking great care of these testimonies and working hard to get them out to the public. There are so many more to thank over the years that I have grown from and served the Lord with; you all mean so very much to me. I love and appreciate every one of you.

CPSIA information can be obtained
at www.ICGtesting.com
Printed in the USA
BVHW091938130423
662312BV00016B/212

9 781662 875793